From Ego to Self
108 Affirmations for Daily Living

Paul Ferrini

Designed & Illustrated by
Susan Linville

ISBN 1-879159-01-5

Manufactured in the United States of America

WHAT IS THE EGO?

Ego is the refusal to see the Source. It is the choice to be separate, which results in conflict. Ego is created in the act of denial. Rejecting its origin, it simultaneously creates its own world of meaning, a world that is dualistic, and inherently destructive, for what it creates it must also destroy.

Ego is not a state of being, but a choice made in each moment. In the present we always have the choice of ego or Self. Ego is established when we seek our own good at the expense of another's. Self is experienced when we recognize our common origin and our shared purpose.

Ego is the movement toward and attachment to the objects of the world. Self is the emancipation from the world and the re-cognition of our "a priori" relationship with each other and with God.

WHAT IS THE SELF?

Self is who we are in our fullness and purity. It can be shared with others, but it is not determined by anything external. When we are in touch with Self, we are aligned with the whole, of which we are part.

Self is a particular manifestation of the totality of being we call God. Each Self inheres in God, manifests from It, and knows itself in relation to It. The ability of one Self to recognize another is identical with its ability to know its Source, for the Source of each is the same.

Self is differentiated from its Source but not cut off from It. Only by recognizing Itself as unlimited by form can it re-connect with the formless, the indivisible totality of being. The expression "God the Father," or "Creator" merely describes the origin of the Self, not the quality of the Source, which can never be described or defined.

MOVING FROM EGO TO SELF

The movement from ego to Self begins with our ability to embrace ourselves totally, exactly as we are. We must accept the ego for what it is: a scared child, trying to protect itself from imagined attack. To that child, attack is always imminent and always real. Trying to convince the child that attack is not real does not work. The child is scared and needs to be comforted and re-assured.

Embracing the ego means embracing the hurt child within. It does not mean that we affirm his distorted perceptions or capitulate to his un-reasonable demands. It simply means that we accept him as worthy and lovable. We listen to his demands and thus begin to diffuse them.

If we refuse to listen to the child, he will take up his stand against us. He will become the angry monster we fear. But we must understand then that this is a self-fulfilling prophesy. The child is only dangerous if we neglect him. When we bring him into our arms again, he begins to heal and grow.

We sometimes forget that this child does not feel loved. He does not feel appreciated as he is. He believes that he must behave or "perform" in some way to win the approval of the adults around him. He is afraid to make mistakes, because he does not want to disappoint others and lose their love. Yet, inevitably, he makes mistakes and judges himself unworthy because of them.

Redeeming the ego means re-connecting the child to the Source of love within. It means teaching him that the struggle for perfection is distorted and misleading. When the child can accept his wordly "imperfection" he can begin to get in touch with his inner "perfection." In this way he learns to give birth to a wholeness and completeness that was always there.

As the inner child is embraced, the fear and separateness which are the trademarks of the ego begin to fade. And with them go a whole series of tragic, alienating, distorted, and manipulative behaviors designed to help the child cope with rejection and refusal.

Gradually, as true Self-acceptance comes, the adult realizes that any rejection he experienced as a child was but a reflection of his inner sense of inadequacy. He can own that now. And he can also own the fact that the love and acceptance of others flows from his ability to love and accept himself as he is.

Recognizing the futility of looking outside of himself for satisfaction, he looks for acceptance within, and so comes back into alignment with his Source. That alignment is his true security and strength. It is also the basis of his compassion. Because he feels affirmed within, he no longer sees his brother's criticism as an attack upon him, but as a cry for acceptance and love.

When we embrace our own inner child, we are not threatened by the ego-displays of others. We no longer need to go head to head in hand to hand combat with others who make judgments about us. We no longer want to be right at any cost. Instead, we seek our peace first, because peace is our strength.

In seeking peace, we find it, for it is our inmost nature. The Self is peaceful. Being "full of peace," we see others out of that inner fullness. Perceptions of fear and lack are ancient history. They are what we saw "through a glass darkly," what we saw as scared children. But now we see "face to face," for now we see through the eyes of love.

HOW TO USE THIS BOOK

The affirmations in this book are designed to help you get in touch with the wisdom of the Self. If you use these affirmations frequently and with proper concentration, they will transform the quality of your life.

Whenever you feel angry, sad, confused, or upset, open the Book and find the affirmation that offers you a new way of viewing your situation. It will help release you from conflict. You will feel yourself move from ego to Self, from fear to love, from sadness to joy. Using the appropriate affirmation when your life calls for it increases your energy, faith, and optimism.

This simple but effective spiritual practice will help you affirm your true Being and re-cognize that Being in others. It will plant the seeds of love which flower in your relationships, and restore your feeling of inner-connectedness with all things.

When I recognize my limited way of thinking, new possibilities emerge in my life.

I can't see who you are
until *I* surrender my expectations of you.

Only because we believe we are separate
do our needs seem to conflict.

$\mathcal{I}$ re-cognize that
my anger, fear, and frustration
are ultimately directed at myself.

*I refuse to blame you or myself.
Instead, I learn to rely on love.*

$\mathcal{T}$he more I justify my judgment of you,
the deeper my guilt.

As soon as *I* recognize my mistake,
I have begun to correct it.

$\mathcal{I}$ can't be happy until $\mathcal{I}$ let go
of my lingering guilt
over mistakes $\mathcal{I}$ have made in the past.

*No matter how much I protest,
I remain responsible
for everything that happens to me.*

Conflicts between us dissolve
when I re-cognize my equality with you.

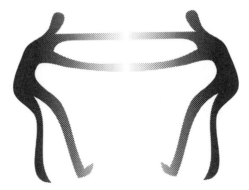

*M*y back is to the wall
only as long as
I'm unwilling to forgive you
or myself.

Only my fear causes me to forget
that a positive outcome can be realized
in any situation.

$\mathcal{I}$f $\mathcal{I}$ have something you don't have,
then it must be an illusion.

*L*ife is a struggle only
when *I* need to interfere
with the way things are.

$\mathcal{L}$oving myself means
I no longer need to be
physically or psychologically
aggressive toward others.

How can I find the truth
if I am busy retaliating
against illusions?

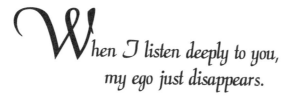

When I listen deeply to you,
my ego just disappears.

*I do not engage in the struggles of the world,
but bring my peace to all situations.*

*M*y
compassion arises
when my ability to love
no longer depends
on how others treat me.

I exclude no one
from my idea of truth or justice.

I am true to myself
when my thoughts, words and deeds
are consistent with my goals.

I practice forgiveness moment to moment,
thereby maintaining and extending my peace.

The apparent differences between us cannot threaten our common origin, nor our equality before God.

Having done all I am able to do,
I relax
and let God do the rest.

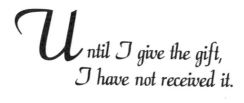

Until I give the gift, I have not received it.

*I accept necessary changes,
even though they may
temporarily disrupt my life.*

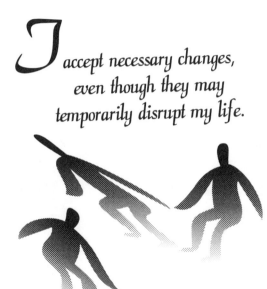

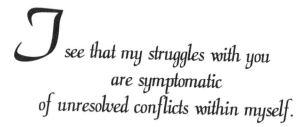

*I see that my struggles with you
are symptomatic
of unresolved conflicts within myself.*

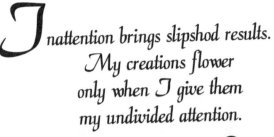

Inattention brings slipshod results.
My creations flower
only when I give them
my undivided attention.

Because I no longer feel superior to you,
I am no longer haunted by
subconscious feelings of inferiority.

$\mathcal{I}$ know in each moment
that $\mathcal{I}$ am free to decide.

I have the courage to face my self-created reality.

I express how *I* feel honestly,
without blaming myself
or attacking you.

$\mathcal{I}$ seem to be lacking what $\mathcal{I}$ need
only because $\mathcal{I}$ desire
what is contrary to my growth.

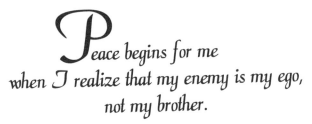

*Peace begins for me
when I realize that my enemy is my ego,
not my brother.*

When I learn to love my brother,
I make peace with my ego too.

$\mathcal{I}$ realize that my growth is compromised
by my neurotic dependency on you,
or yours on me.

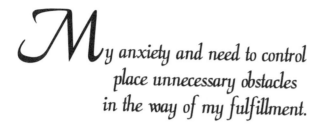

*M*y anxiety and need to control
place unnecessary obstacles
in the way of my fulfillment.

I stay focused in the present,
letting go of my perceptions of the past
and my expectations of the future.

When I surrender my preferences,
I see the true meaning
of the events unfolding in my life.

*A*ny situation beyond my control
offers me the opportunity to love
and to trust.

I respect and identify with all living things.

53

$\mathcal{E}$very day I find a way to make peace with the people in my life.

I know that anything is possible
    if my desire for it is strong
and it is in harmony with who I am.

I see the destructive quality
of all criticism
and so refrain from it
as an exercise in non-violence.

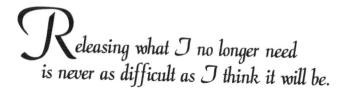

*Releasing what I no longer need
is never as difficult as I think it will be.*

*Accepting others as they are
is always enough.*

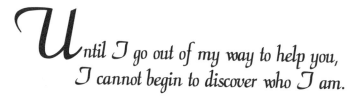

Until I go out of my way to help you, I cannot begin to discover who I am.

$\mathcal{E}$ ven the greatest risks
merely free me from imagined boundaries.

When I am quiet, relaxed, and centered,
I see and respond clearly to life.

$\mathcal{E}$very day I take care of my body, challenge my mind, and establish my peace.

I trust my intuition
as much as I trust my analytical thinking.

Whenever I am in doubt,
I remember that there is a valid reason
for everything that happens.

I realize that my peace is perfect
and available to me at all times.

$\mathcal{N}$othing can stand
in the way of my happiness,
unless I give it permission
to do so.

Whenever I'm afraid to give something,
I remember that everything I have
is borrowed from the infinite supply,
including my body
and the events & circumstances of my life.

$\mathcal{I}$ see that my fulfillment is limited
by what $\mathcal{I}$ think $\mathcal{I}$ own, control, or possess.

$\mathcal{I}$ realize that attack and counter-attack
are the same thing.

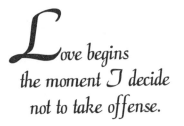

Love begins
the moment I decide
not to take offense.

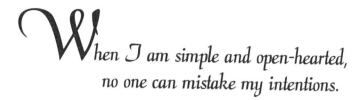

When I am simple and open-hearted,
no one can mistake my intentions.

I am without flaws
when *I* am transparent:
hiding nothing,
revealing everything.

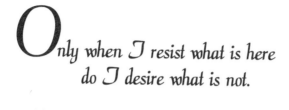

Only when $\mathcal{I}$ resist what is here
do $\mathcal{I}$ desire what is not.

$\mathcal{I}$ am fair and even-handed,
even when others choose not to be.

*F*ear does not enter
into the decisions *I* make.

$\mathcal{I}$ freely give what $\mathcal{I}$ have in abundance,
and ask without embarrassment
for what $\mathcal{I}$ genuinely need.

I don't need to think about tomorrow.
I know that my needs are being met right now.

I can no longer justify
refusing anyone.

$\mathcal{I}$ don't procrastinate
or make promises $\mathcal{I}$ can't keep.
$\mathcal{I}$ tell you when $\mathcal{I}$ can't meet
your expectations.

Not choosing betrays
my power to create what I want.

*Injustice is an illusion.
I cannot be treated unfairly.*

$\mathcal{I}$ am not afraid to decide,
nor compelled to decide before $\mathcal{I}$ am ready.

The people in my life
reflect back to me
the choices I have made.

*I'd rather say "I don't know"
than pretend to know when I don't.*

I am not content with what I know,
nor foolish enough to think
that I must know everything.

Truth has no exceptions,
nor does Forgiveness.

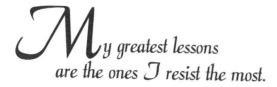

My greatest lessons
are the ones I resist the most.

I don't have to be a saint.
I just need to realize that *I'm* unhappy
when *I'm* not loving you.

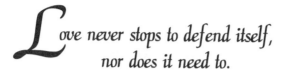

*L*ove never stops to defend itself,
nor does it need to.

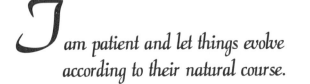

$\mathcal{I}$ am patient and let things evolve according to their natural course.

My inner guidance means nothing
if I do not rely on it
in times of difficulty.

I realize that *I* can't forgive you
before forgiving myself.

*The more we share,
the more we experience
our wholeness.*

$\mathcal{I}$ always feel cut off
from the love $\mathcal{I}$ reject.

When I am open,
so are the gates of heaven.

*Trust is my greatest ally;
suspicion my greatest foe.*

*What I see in you
is what I get.*

There is a place love touches
where the body cannot go.

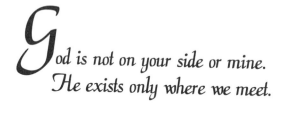

God is not on your side or mine. He exists only where we meet.

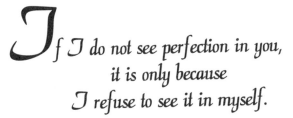

*I*f I do not see perfection in you,
it is only because
I refuse to see it in myself.

Clarity is lost
as soon as judgment arises.

*Love sees all things
equal & alike.*

*C*hanges may appear at the surface,
but spirit rests in the center,
which is unchanging.

*Present needs cannot be met
by the solutions of the past.*

$\mathcal{B}$oth past and future are limited.
Only this moment is whole and free.

$\mathcal{N}$o matter how much $\mathcal{I}$ plan,
$\mathcal{I}$ never know where $\mathcal{I}$'m going
until $\mathcal{I}$ get there.

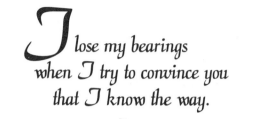

I lose my bearings
when *I* try to convince you
that *I* know the way.

*I*t is hard to see the Self
when ego is always putting itself first.

When I'm in touch with my bliss,
no one can betray me.

*N*ow that you are free,
my chains have also been removed.

$\mathcal{D}$eath is as close to me now
as it will ever be.

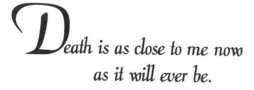

*G*od is not responsible
for my inability to find Him.

The more we listen,
the more profound the silence gets.

I move out of ego traffic
when *I* let go of my opinions
and just do the best *I* can.

The more I push,
the more pressure I put
on myself.

$\mathcal{P}$rotecting you is just a clever way
of hiding the truth from myself.

When I am completely here,
no one tries to pin me down.

Sometimes I get more confused
explaining things
than just leaving them be.

Without the world to confirm it,
the ego just falls away.

When Self is realized,
the perception of inequality
ceases to be.

P aul Ferrini is the author of numerous books which help us heal the emotional body and embrace a spirituality grounded in the real challenges of daily life. Paul's work is heart-centered and experiential, empowering us to move through our fear and shame and share who we are authentically with others. Paul Ferrini founded and edited *Miracles Magazine*, a publication devoted to telling Miracle

Stories offering hope and inspiration to all of us. Paul's conferences, retreats and *Affinity Group Process* have helped thousands of people deepen their practice of forgiveness and open their hearts to the Divine presence in themselves and others. For more information on Paul's workshops and retreats or *The Affinity Group Process*, contact Heartways Press, P.O. Box 181, South Deerfield, MA 01373 or call 413-665-0555.

Passionate Poems and a Love Story

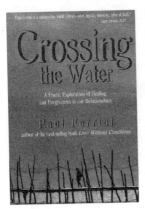

Crossing The Water
Poems About Healing and Forgiveness in Our
Relationships by Paul Ferrini

ISBN 1-879159-25-2
$9.95
96 pages, paperback

The time for healing and reconciliation has come, Ferrini
writes. Our relationships help us heal childhood wounds,
walk through our deepest fears, and cross over the water
of our emotional pain. Just as the rocks in the river are
pounded and caressed to rounded stone, the rough edges of our personalities are
worn smooth in the context of a committed relationship. If we can keep our hearts
open, we can heal together, experience genuine equality, and discover what it
means to give and receive love without conditions.

Miracle of Love, Reflections of the Christ Mind, Part III by Paul Ferrini

ISBN 1-879159-23-6
$12.95, 192 pages, paperback

Many people say that this latest volume of the Christ Mind series is the best yet. Jesus tells us:"I was born to a simple woman in a barn. She was no more a virgin than your mother was." Moreover, he tells us, the virgin birth is not the only myth surrounding his life and teaching. So are the concepts of vicarious atonement and physical resurrection. Relentlessly, the master tears down the rigid dogma and hierarchical teachings that obscure his simple message of love and forgiveness. He encourages us to take him down from the pedestal and the cross and see him as an equal brother who found the way out of suffering by opening his heart totally. We too can open our hearts and find peace and happiness. "The power of love will make miracles in your life as wonderful as any attributed to me," he tells us. "Your birth into this embodiment is no less holy than mine. The love that you extend to others is no less important than the love I extend to you."

Now Finally our Bestselling Title on Audio Tape

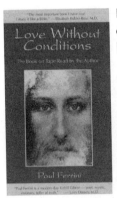

Love Without Conditions, Reflections
of the Christ Mind, Part I
by Paul Ferrini

The Book on Tape
Read by the Author
2 Cassettes,
Approximately 3.25 hours

ISBN 1-879159-24-4
$19.95

Now on audio tape: the incredible book from Jesus calling us to awaken to our own Christhood. Listen to this gentle, profound, book while driving in your car or before going to sleep at night. Elisabeth Kubler-Ross calls this "the most important book I have read. I study it like a Bible." Find out for yourself how this amazing book has helped thousands of people understand the radical teachings of the master and begin to integrate these teachings into their lives.

• Waking Up Together Illuminations on the Road to Nowhere

There comes a time for all of us when the outer destinations no longer satisfy and we finally understand that the love and happiness we seek cannot be found outside of us. It must be found in our own hearts, on the other side of our pain. "The Road to Nowhere is the path through your heart. It is not a journey of escape. It is a journey through your pain to end the pain of separation."

This book makes it clear that we can no longer rely on outer teachers or teachings to find our spiritual identity. Nor can we find who we are in relationships where boundaries are blurred and one person makes decisions for another. If we want to be authentic, we can't allow anyone else to be an authority for us, nor can we allow ourselves to be an authority for another person.

Authentic relationships happen between equal partners who take responsibility for their own consciousness and experience. When their buttons are pushed, they are willing to look at the obstacles they have erected to the experience of love and acceptance. As they understand and surrender the false ideas and emotional reactions that create separation, genuine intimacy becomes possible, and the sacred dimension of the relationship is born. 216 pp. paper ISBN 1-879159-17-1 $14.95

• The Ecstatic Moment: A Practical Manual for Opening Your Heart and Staying in It.

A simple, power-packed guide that helps us take appropriate responsibility for our experience and establish healthy boundaries with others. Part II contains many helpful exercises and meditations that teach us to stay centered, clear and open in heart and mind. The Affinity Group Process and other group practices help us learn important listening and communication skills that can transform our troubled relationships. Once you have read this book, you will keep it in your briefcase or on your bedside table, referring to it often. You will not find a more practical, down to earth guide to contemporary spirituality. You will want to order copies for all your friends. 128 pp. paper ISBN 1-879159-18-X $10.95

• The Silence of the Heart Reflections of the Christ Mind, Part 2
A powerful sequel to *Love Without Conditions*. John Bradshaw says: "with deep insight and sparkling clarity, this book demonstrates that the roots of all abuse are to be found in our own self-betrayal. Paul Ferrini leads us skillfully and courageously beyond shame, blame, and attachment to our wounds into the depths of self-forgiveness...a must read for all people who are ready to take responsibility for their own healing." 218 pp. paper.   ISBN 1-879159-16-3 $14.95

• **Love Without Conditions:**
Reflections of the Christ Mind - Part I
An incredible book from Jesus calling us to awaken to our Christhood. Rarely has any book conveyed the teachings of the master in such a simple but profound manner. This book will help you to bring your understanding from the head to the heart so that you can model the teachings of love and forgiveness in your daily life. 192 pp. paper ISBN 1-879159-15-15 $12.00

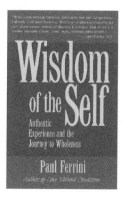

• **The Wisdom of the Self**
This ground-breaking book explores our authentic experience and our journey to wholeness. "Your life is your spiritual path. Don't be quick to abandon it for promises of bigger and better experiences. You are getting exactly the experiences you need to grow. If your growth seems too slow or uneventful for you, it is because you have not fully embraced the situations and relationships at hand…To know the Self is to allow everything, to embrace the totality of who we are, all that we think and feel, all of our fear, all of our love." 229 pp. paper ISBN 1-879159-14-7 $12.00

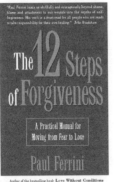

• The Twelve Steps of Forgiveness

A practical manual for healing ourselves and our relationships. This book gives us a step-by-step process for moving through our fears, projections, judgments, and guilt so that we can take responsibility for creating the life we want. With great gentleness, we learn to embrace our lessons and to find equality with others. A must read for all in recovery and others seeking spiritual wholeness. 128 pp. paper ISBN 1-879159-10-4 $10.00

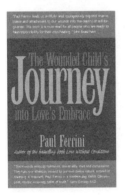

• The Wounded Child's Journey Into Love's Embrace

This book explores a healing process in which we confront our deep-seated guilt and fear, bringing love and forgiveness to the wounded child within. By surrendering our judgments of self and others, we overcome feelings of separation and dismantle co-dependent patterns that restrict our self-expression and ability to give and receive love. 225pp. paper ISBN 1-879159-06-6 $12.00

• The Bridge to Reality

A Heart-Centered Approach to *A Course in Miracles* and the Process of Inner Healing. Sharing his experiences of spiritual awakening, Paul emphasizes self-acceptance and forgiveness as cornerstones of spiritual practice. Presented with beautiful photos, this book conveys the essence of *The Course* as it is lived in daily life. 192 pp. paper ISBN 1-879159-03-1 $12.00

• From Ego to Self

108 illustrated affirmations designed to offer you a new way of viewing conflict situations so that you can overcome negative thinking and bring more energy, faith and optimism into your life. 128 pp. paper ISBN 1-879159-01-5 $10.00

• Virtues of The Way
A lyrical work of contemporary scripture reminiscent of the Tao Te Ching. Beautifully illustrated, this inspirational book will help you cultivate the spiritual values required to fulfill your creative purpose and live in harmony with others. 64 pp. paper ISBN 1-879159-02-3 $7.50

• The Body of Truth
A crystal clear introduction to the universal teachings of love and forgiveness. This book traces all forms of suffering to negative attitudes and false beliefs, which we have the ability to transform. 64 pp. paper ISBN 1-879159-02-3 $7.50

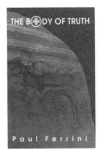

• Available Light
Inspirational, passionate poems dealing with the work of inner integration, love and relationships, death and re-birth, loss and abundance, life purpose and the reality of spiritual vision. 128 pp. paper ISBN 1-879159-05-8 $12.00

Poetry and Guided Meditation Tapes
by Paul Ferrini

The Poetry of the Soul

With its heartfelt combination of sensuality and spirituality, Paul Ferrini's poetry has been compared to the poetry of Rumi. These luminous poems demonstrate why Paul Ferrini is first a poet, a lover and a mystic. Come to this feast of the beloved with an open heart and open ears. With Suzi Kesler on piano. $10.00 ISBN 1-879159-26-0

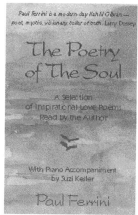

The Circle of Healing

The meditation and healing tape that many of you have been seeking. This gentle meditation opens the heart to love's presence and extends that love to all the beings in your experience. A powerful tape with inspirational piano accompaniment by Michael Gray. ISBN 1-879159-08-2 $10.00

Healing the Wounded Child

A potent healing tape that accesses old feelings of pain, fragmentation, self-judgment and separation and brings them into the light of conscious awareness and acceptance. Side two includes a hauntingly beautiful "inner child" reading from *The Bridge to Reality* with piano accompaniment by Michael Gray. ISBN 1-879159-11-2 $10.00

Forgiveness: Returning to the Original Blessing

A self healing tape that helps us accept and learn from the mistakes we have made in the past. By letting go of our judgments and ending our ego-based search for perfection, we can bring our darkness to the light, dissolving anger, guilt, and shame. Piano accompaniment by Michael Gray. ISBN 1-879159-12-0 $10.00

Paul Ferrini Talks and Workshop Tapes

Answering Our Own Call for Love
*A Sermon given at the Pacific Church of
Religious Science in San Diego, CA 11/97*

Paul tells the story of his own spiritual awakening, his
Atheist upbringing, and how he began to open to the
presence of God and his connection with Jesus and the
Christ Mind teaching. In a very clear, heart-felt way, Paul
presents to us the spiritual path of love, acceptance, and
forgiveness. Also available on videotape. 1 Cassette
$10.00 ISBN 1-879159-33-3

The Ecstatic Moment *A workshop given by Paul in Los Angeles
at the Agape International Center of Truth, May, 1997*

Shows us how we can be with our pain compassionately and learn to nurture the
light within ourselves, even when it appears that we are walking through darkness.
Discusses subjects such as living in the present, acceptance, not fixing self or others,
being with our discomfort and learning that we are lovable as we are. *1 Cassette
$10.00 ISBN 1-879159-27-9*

Honoring Self and Other *A Workshop at the Pacific Church of Religious Science in San Diego, November, 1997*

Helps us understand the importance of not betraying ourselves in our relationships with others. Focuses on understanding healthy boundaries, setting limits, and saying no to others in a loving way. Real life examples include a woman who is married to a man who is chronically critical of her, and a gay man who wants to tell his judgmental parents that he has AIDS. *1 Cassette $10.00 ISBN 1-879159-34-1*

Seek First the Kingdom *Two Sunday Messages given by Paul: the first in May, 1997 in Los Angeles at the Agape Int'l. Center of Truth, and the second in September, 1997 in Portland, OR at the Unity Church.*

Discusses the words of Jesus in the Sermon on the Mount: "Seek first the kingdom and all else will be added to you." Helps us understand how we create the inner temple by learning to hold our judgments of self and other more compassionately. The love of God flows through our love and acceptance of ourselves. As we establish our connection to the divine within ourselves, we don't need to look outside of ourselves for love and acceptance. Includes fabulous music by The Agape Choir and Band. *1 Cassette $10.00 ISBN 1-879159-30-9*

Ending the Betrayal of the Self
A Workshop given by Paul at the Learning Annex in Toronto, April, 1997

A roadmap for integrating the opposing voices in our psyche so that we can experience our own wholeness. Delineates what our responsibility is and isn't in our relationships with others, and helps us learn to set clear, firm, but loving boundaries. Our relationships can become areas of sharing and fulfillment, rather than mutual invitations to co-dependency and self betrayal. *2 Cassettes $16.95 ISBN 1-879159-28-7*

Relationships: Changing Past Patterns *A Talk with Questions and Answers Given at the Redondo Beach Church of Religious Science, 11/97*

Begins with a Christ Mind talk describing the link between learning to love and accept ourselves and learning to love and accept others. Helps us understand how we are invested in the past and continue to replay our old relationship stories. Helps us get clear on what we want and understand how to be faithful to it. By being totally committed to ourselves, we give birth to the beloved within and also without. Includes an in-depth discussion about meditation, awareness, hearing our inner voice, and the Affinity Group Process. *2 Cassettes $16.95 ISBN 1-879159-32-5*

Relationship As a Spiritual Path *A workshop given by Paul in Los Angeles at the Agape Int'l. Center of Truth, May, 1997*

Explores concrete ways in which we can develop a relationship with ourselves and learn to take responsibility for our own experience, instead of blaming others for our perceived unworthiness. Also discussed: accepting our differences, the new paradigm of relationship, the myth of the perfect partner, telling our truth, compassion vs. rescuing, the unavailable partner, abandonment issues, negotiating needs, when to say no, when to stay and work on a relationship and when to leave. *2 Cassettes $16.95 ISBN 1-879159-29-5*

Opening to Christ Consciousness *A Talk with Questions & Answers at Unity Church, Tustin, CA November, 1997*

Begins with a Christ Mind talk giving us a clear picture of how the divine spark dwells within each of us and how we can open up to God-consciousness on a regular basis. Deals with letting go and forgiveness in our relationships with our parents, our children and our partners. A joyful, funny, and scintillating tape you will want to listen to many times. Also available on videotape. *2 Cassettes $16.95 ISBN 1-879159-31-7*

Risen Christ Posters and Notecards

Set of 8 Notecards
with Envelopes
ISBN 1-879159-20-1 $10.00

11"x17" Poster
suitable for framing
ISBN 1-879159-19-8 $10.00

8.5"x11" Poster
suitable for framing
ISBN 1-879159-21-X $5.00

Set of 8 Notecards
with Envelopes
ISBN 1-879159-22-8 $10.00

Coming in Early 1998

Return to the Garden
Part IV of the Reflections of
The Christ Mind Series.

Living in the Heart
The Affinity Process and the Path of
Unconditional Love and Acceptance

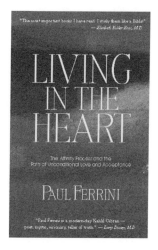

Heartways Press Order Form

Name_____

Address_____

City _____State _____Zip _____

Phone _____

BOOKS BY PAUL FERRINI

Return to the Garden ($12.95) . . . . _____
Living in the Heart ($10.95) . . . . _____
Miracle of Love ($12.95) . . . . _____
Crossing the Water ($9.95) . . . . _____
Waking Up Together ($14.95) . . . . _____
The Ecstatic Moment ($10.95) . . . . _____
The Silence of the Heart ($14.95) . . . . _____
Love Without Conditions ($12.00) . . . . _____
The Wisdom of the Self ($12.00) . . . . _____
The Twelve Steps of Forgiveness ($10.00) . . . . _____
The Circle of Atonement ($12.00) . . . . _____
The Bridge to Reality ($12.00) . . . . _____
From Ego to Self ($10.00) . . . . _____
Virtues of the Way ($7.50) . . . . _____
The Body of Truth ($7.50) . . . . _____
Available Light ($10.00) . . . . _____

AUDIO TAPES

The Circle of Healing ($10.00). . . . . _____
Healing the Wounded Child ($10.00) . . . . _____
Forgiveness: Returning to the Original Blessing ($10.00) . . . . _____
The Poetry of the Soul ($10.00) . . . . _____
Seek First the Kingdom ($10.00) . . . . _____
Answering Our Own Call for Love ($10.00) . . . . _____
The Ecstatic Moment ($10.00) . . . . _____
Honoring Self and Other ($10.00) . . . . _____
Love Without Conditions ($19.95) 2 tapes . . . . _____
Ending the Betrayal of the Self ($16.95) 2 tapes . . . . _____
Relationships: Changing Past Patterns ($16.95) 2 tapes . . . . _____
Relationship As a Spiritual Path ($16.95) 2 tapes . . . . _____
Opening to Christ Consciousness ($16.95) 2 tapes . . . . _____

POSTERS AND NOTECARDS

Risen Christ Poster 11"x17" ($10.00). . . . . _____
Ecstatic Moment Poster 8.5"x11" ($5.00). . . . . _____
Risen Christ Notecards with envelopes 8/pkg ($10.00). _____
Ecstatic Moment Notecards with envelopes 8/pkg ($10.00) . . . . _____

SHIPPING

($2.00 for first item, $1.00 each additional item.
Add additional $1.00 for first class postage.) _____
MA residents please add 5% sales tax. _____

TOTAL $_____

Please allow 1-2 weeks for delivery

Send Order To: Heartways Press
P. O. Box 181, South Deerfield, MA 01373
413-665-0555 • 413-665-4565 (fax)
Toll free: 1-888-HARTWAY